CW01431486

The
Beautiful Mystery

A Collection of Poems to
Inspire Your Daily Journey

Aldinah Acibo

BookLeaf
Publishing

The Soul, A Beautiful Mystery

A Collection of Poems to Inspire Your Daily Journey © 2023 Aldinah Acibo

Presentation by *BookLeaf Publishing*

Web: www.bookleafpub.com

E-mail: info@bookleafpub.com

ISBN: 9789357213325

First edition 2023

The Soul, A Beautiful Mystery

Remember the day when you feel different
A day when you asked yourself "WHO AM I ?"
That was the day when you remembered WHO
YOU ARE
A DIVINE being of LIGHT
A VESSEL through which GOD can work

As You FEEL it, Then You BELIEVE IT

It is easy to believe something when you can see
it with your physical eyes
But what we see physically are the illusions
What is unseen, but felt by the soul is the REAL
one
Open up your spiritual eye
And see what reality is

Unconditional Love, Divine Gift

Feel the beat of your heart
Have you listen to its call?
Listen more and you will understand
Every beat is the Divine's UNCONDITIONAL
LOVE

The Guiding Lights

Have you look up the night sky?
See those tiny bright lights
You are one of them
They are up there
But you are here
Share that light from within

When you HEAL, GAIA Heals

As we are One with the Earth
Our energy affects her energy
Our rage is her rage
Our calmness is her calmness
When something strange is happening
Find the answer by going within

The SEA as you See it

The waves can be calm or raging
It depends on what you are feeling
The sea is always conforting
But be mindful of the energy you are giving

Solitude

How wonderful it is
To live in the present bliss
Appreciating the moment of ease
Communing with the DIVINE in perfect BLISS

Fly High

Birds are soaring high
Reminding us to let out a sigh
Relishing the freedom given
As our thoughts can create our own heaven

White Butterfly

How pure the colour you have
You fly as elegant as a soft wave
Doing your mission in a subtle way
As you kiss each flower with a sway

The Sun

Rising up in the sky
Lighting up the birds flying by
How soothing to feel your warm
It makes my soul feel calm

Fresh

A big shift has arrived
The freshness cannot be denied
Each morning is a GOLDEN glow
With inspirations to let it flow

Two Birds Flying

Two Birds flying together
And showing care for each other
Enjoying the freedom in the moment
As they gaze each other with contentment
They can fly through the highs and lows
As long as they are flying in twos

Train Of Life

The journey of life is like a train
People on board can choose to go or remain
But everyone has a significant role to play
So be grateful and don't dismay

Keep Going

Looking at the hilltop can be overwhelming
You can never fathom what you are feeling
But you want to discover life's meaning
So you take the first step and keep going

When Your Eyes Speak

Everytime our eyes met are truly divine
I can feel the pureness when your eyes look to
mine
Surely you know the language of my Soul
It ignites a unique spark and makes me grateful

Anchoring The Lights

The Light from the Central Sun
Bringing Life to everyone
But not all are consciously aware of its
magnificence
Each ray is meant to awaken our senses

Being still in the moment
While gazing at the sunset with excitement
Is what it takes to integrate this Energy
The vital Life Force that we should fully
embody

Soul Oneness

As we shed the ego aspect of self
We learn to live in this world
Knowing that there is more than what we can
see
We recognize others to their Soul level
We detach from giving them label
We know that feeling of loneliness is an illusion
We focus on Oneness as our Mission

Love And Light

When you are awaken to Who You truly are in
your true essence
You cannot go back to sleep and pretend that
your Soul is not awake
Accept your Soul Essence
Integrate the power within You
For you are chosen to enlighten the world and its
humanity
Be the Love and Light to lead the Unity

Seeking Honesty

We always want honesty from others
But not everyone is honest with himself
Have you asked that person in the mirror first?
What does your Soul is calling you to do?
Are you doing things because of joy?

Honesty can only be found
If you are honest with yourself first
Be honest on what ignites your passion
Be honest on what you are feeling
Your Soul deserves that honesty

Two Souls Unite

Old Souls that had gone through many lifetimes
Each one had gone through healing and growth
It was not easy for both to RISE ABOVE human
emotions
But every experience is essential for their Soul
mission
Now the time has come for these two Souls to
Unite
And share to the world their combined Love and
Light

Take Flight

It is time for you to get out of the cocoon
Marvel Yourself with those magical wings
Use them to take the quantum leap of faith
You have been prepared for this moment
So spread your wings and TAKE FLIGHT

Milton Keynes UK
Ingram Content Group UK Ltd.
UKHW020329100524
442467UK00012B/249

9 789357 213325